From the author of Revelation

JOHN BURTON

COVENS
IN THE CHURCH

God's plan to change the world is under attack...from within.

To Miles Anderson. A friend and brother who has battled with me in amazing warfare against the enemy's camp with passion, love and loyalty.

John Burton is a church planter, conference speaker and author with a mandate to see the fire of God's presence invade cities and nations. He planted Revolution Church in Manitou Springs, Colorado and Revival Church in Detroit, Michigan.

John's ministry style could be described as wildly passionate, engaging, humorous and loaded with the flow and power of the Holy Spirit.

The prevailing theme of the ministry God has given John revolves around the topic of 'being with God'. Where God is, things happen. In His presence, the place where He is, is the fullness of joy. As we discover the wonderful mystery of walking in the Spirit, praying always and making aggressive strides in faith, life becomes incredible!

It truly is an experience in the invisible realm. As we tangibly experience God through deep and active prayer we are interacting 'in the Spirit'. As we walk by faith and understand how amazing a Holy Spirit driven life is, being a believer quickly becomes the greatest adventure on earth!

John is currently focused on teaching, consulting, writing and ministering to churches. If you would like to invite John to speak at your church, conference, camp or other event, please visit www.johnburton.net.

COVENS IN THE CHURCH

Luke 7:8 For I also am a man placed under authority, having soldiers under me. And I say to one, 'Go,' and he goes; and to another, 'Come,' and he comes; and to my servant, 'Do this,' and he does it."

The centurion was much like God's appointed apostles, prophets, teachers, small group leaders and Sunday school teachers of today. He acknowledged he was a man both under authority and one with authority over others.

As the leader of Revolution House of Prayer I have people who God has appointed as my authority. We call them overseers and they are leaders of ministries and people with a mature walk with the Lord. Like the centurion, I am a man under authority.

Let's say, for example, I, along with the leadership of Revolution, decide to hold a conference. We go through the tedious process of securing guest speakers and figuring out how to administrate the event. We spend thousands of dollars promoting the conference on TV, radio and in print. I am a key part of the process as well as the actual event. I'll be teaching in several of the workshops and facilitating the week of activities. A week before the conference I receive a phone call from one of my overseers. He tells me he needs me to fly to Alabama to help a church work through a transition from one pastor to another. Their previous pastor just repented of indiscretion and resigned suddenly. The problem? It's during the same week as my conference. I would have a dilemma.

Honestly, I don't want to go to Alabama. In addition to the upcoming conference I have a wedding to officiate among other important tasks. My integrity and reputation, along with my own personal comfort would be at stake. What's the correct approach to take?

- Refuse to mention my disagreement with my overseer with anybody–including my wife. There is power of life and death in the tongue. Out of the abundance of the heart the mouth speaks. I'd have to allow God to break me and cause me to have a pure heart in this matter.
- Put to death any of my own desires and prepare to surrender to the wishes of my overseer however inconvenient they may be.
- Meet with my overseer and honestly share all of the concerns and issues at stake. Inform him that I'd prefer not to go and if he could find someone else, I'd really appreciate it.
- Submit. After a healthy conversation, my overseer states that he appreciates my concerns but he still needs me to go. So, I go.

I don't have to pray about my decision. I don't have to talk with anybody else. I have no option according to God's established government in my life. I fly to Alabama with a smile on my face. God's authority has spoken.

The enemy has caused many to believe that we can't experience freedom while being submitted. This is simply not true.

Freedom from authority is rebellion.
Freedom in the absence of authority is anarchy.
Freedom under authority is liberty.

The process of response to my leader described above not only must take place between a pastor and his overseers, but also between a youth pastor and his pastor. Also, between the ministers in the pews and their leaders. We'll eventually see the city Church established once again and pastors will be submitting to apostles in their city. It's a process that is quite foreign to most.

So, what is the big idea here? It's not to validate poor leadership. It's to ensure that we go through the proper processes in the face of disagreement so as to keep all of us as holy soldiers in position.

Why is it so critical that this sensitive issue be discussed? I'm fully aware that many have been wounded by poor leaders in their lives. While some difficult points will be discussed over the next several pages, it must be made clear now that while God desires leaders to serve with great love, humility, passion and care, there are some in the body who simply do not do so. *While God will hold those leaders deeply accountable for their leadership, God will hold the rest of us accountable for how we respond to them.* Do we serve from a position of great love, humility, passion and care–or not?

Further, the reason this issue must be addressed is primarily for the purpose of fulfilled missions. As you are reading the rest of this book, keep this in mind. Simply, church body life is hard, demanding, irritating and a struggle at times. Any family goes through seasons just like that. However, there is a mission for each local church, and those local and regional missions will serve the greater global mission.

The call is not to validate *poor* leadership. It's to validate leaders who, in their weakness, were positioned by God. It's to ensure that we go through the proper processes in the face of disagreement so as to keep all of us as holy soldiers in position. We simply must serve the greater mission in love and mature to the place where we can trust an infallible God, who is the one who actually appointed our leaders. We are to allow God to work with and through those leaders, who are without question weak and fallible (as we all are). If we don't, the greater mission of the church is compromised. A failed mission at this stage of Church history is not an option, and we must weather some mighty storms if we are to succeed.

INDEPENDENCE, SELF-GOVERNMENT & CONTROL

Nearly twenty years ago something terrible happened in the national church that has made it incredibly difficult for missions from God to be started much less fulfilled. Allow me to share a first hand experience that will shed light on this topic:

In 1988 something new was introduced to the church in America, and people from all walks of Christian life–pillars of the Church, new believers and everyone in between–embraced it like an intimate lover. It was the answer to a prayer.

With this 'new thing' came the promise of protection for every man and woman who aligned with it. It promised power and freedom from abuse and tyranny.

What was this new thing? *It was possibly the largest army of demons ever released on the modern Church.* Their names were Lawlessness, Self-government and Independence. Their master is most probably named Control. It is a spirit of witchcraft and it has been embraced for nearly 20 years now.

In 1988, I was a student at Jimmy Swaggart Bible College. I watched first hand how the enemy could not only bring down arguably the most effective God-ordained ministry of its time, but how he could radically change the course of Church history for his benefit.

I'll never forget my introduction to the 'discerning of spirits'. I don't know that I'll ever be able to fully explain this, as it's deeply personal and spiritual, but I will at least try. As I stepped on the campus of JSBC my life started to change almost immediately. I was feeling a bizarre range of emotions and a deep and weighty blanket of oppression. Before you leap ahead too far in the story, let me make this disclaimer:

I don't believe this oppression was because of the impending fall of Jimmy Swaggart alone. Not even close.

After several months of dealing with this strange new 'illness' alone, I sought out help. I remember going to someone in the dorm who seemed to have a deep and close walk with the Lord. Every day I was living in a strange and foggy reality. I was becoming numb to life. I was becoming fearful and deeply insecure. I felt as if I had lost freedom and liberty. Yet, it was all nonsensical. I was experiencing this never ending oppression every moment of my life for no obvious reason.

I did my best to share what was happening to me with this individual. I didn't know if it was spiritual or physiological. I wondered if the tangible and seemingly physical weight on my mind and the continual feeling of suffocation was because of some strange medical or physical issue. I was never more alone. I was losing hope. I still remember this person's response to me. "I don't know what it could be, brother." That's it. I was still alone.

My introduction into the reality of the spirit realm continued one day when I drove south from the campus in Baton Rouge for about an hour to the city of New Orleans. I had never experienced anything like this in my life. It was as if I was walking on the bottom of a swimming pool. I could actually feel the spiritual atmosphere. The spirit of witchcraft, though I didn't know what to call it at the time, was swirling around me like a whirlwind. The crushing heaviness that I carried day after day was more intense than ever. I felt sick.

This indescribable oppression was the result of a massive strategy of the enemy, and I was in the very center of a nest of demons who had gathered to violently assault the Church worldwide–*all with the agreement of many in the Church itself.*

February 21st, 1988 was a day that changed the church as we knew it. Jim Bakker had already fallen, and mistrust was in the process of taking root in the lives of believers across the nation. I was at Jimmy Swaggart's confession at Family Worship Center in Baton Rouge, Louisiana on that fateful day. Cameras and nationally known news men and women were positioned everywhere. The atmosphere was circus-like. Jimmy Swaggart famously admitted he had sinned and at that very moment all of the forces of hell were released on the Church around the world. It was a covert operation wittingly covered by a much less important overt event that had the attention of the world.

"I'll never be able to trust him."

Shortly after that event I was downtown Baton Rouge evangelizing on the streets. I approached a young, African-American who appeared rough and intimidating–like he could have easily been a member of a gang. He looked very threatening, yet I had already experienced some miraculous moments while witnessing in that area in the past, and my faith was high. It was late at night, and there I was sharing the love of Jesus with this young man. I expected him to laugh and mock me, but he didn't. He asked me why we were out there. I told him we wanted to share God's love with people. He then asked where we were from. I nervously told him I was a student at Jimmy Swaggart Bible College. I was bracing myself for anything from laughter to violence from this young man. I got neither. He hung his head low. What he said next has resounded inside of me ever since.

"I used to watch that man on TV. Many times I almost got on my knees and said that prayer with him. Now I know I'll never say that prayer. *I'll never be able to trust him.*"

Much damage was done that year. Trust was violated. Legions from hell were released. People were hurt. But, let me say this loud and clear–the response of many believers after this event was tragic! It was devastating.

That response has nearly destroyed the Church's forward progress. Missions from God have been aborted or ignored and many people have gone to hell, not because of what Jimmy Swaggart and Jim Bakker did, but because of the new found lack of trust that many in the Church willingly embraced.

The monster of personal opinion was showing its teeth as scrutiny and criticism became acceptable in the minds of believers.

People heard a knock on their door that year. Demonic spirits were released from their nest in Baton Rouge to homes of believers around the world. They were selling their services to disappointed and disillusioned Christians who were fed up with untrustworthy leaders. The sales job was remarkable as so many people of God aligned themselves with demonic salesmen who offered them some free gifts. What were these gifts? Freely given and eagerly received alliances with evil spirits of Independence, Self-government and Lawlessness. *These 'spiritual gifts' were masquerading as freedom from control, though they were themselves assigned by the very spirit of control.* The strong spirits of witchcraft and control had won the battle–and we're still reeling from its effects. Control was offered and the Church moved into a tragic new season that has had horrific effects.

Spontaneously, across the nation and the world, covens of Christians who entertained spirits of Self-government, Independence and Control were established in homes and churches.

The monster of personal opinion was showing its teeth as scrutiny and criticism became acceptable in the minds of believers. People who were once submitted and in love with those God placed in their lives made the conscious decision to turn the tables–*now they were the authority and it was time for their leaders to submit to their plans, ideas, demands and desires.* If they didn't, these people, who were now operating in the spirit of Independence, would assume rule of their lives and remove themselves to find another church, gossip or even attempt to overthrow. Demons were now manipulating churches and individuals from coast to coast—all while they read their Bibles and sang their hymns.

> *Note: At the end of this book I briefly discuss this week's sad news of the resignation of my friend Ted Haggard here in Colorado Springs. We are once again in a place of testing—will covens be started in our nation, or have we learned an important lesson? Keep this recent and strangely similar event in mind as you continue to consider this perspective that has been developing in me for a number of years.*

OUR RELATIONSHIP WITH AUTHORITY

There is a reformation coming to the western Church–and it will bother and challenge our minds and especially our flesh to the very deepest places.

God is highlighting and establishing His government on the earth–His Kingdom. That is why we pray, *"Thy Kingdom come, thy will be done."* God has an end-time will. His Kingdom is coming to the planet, and there are groups and types of people that will be brought to a place of decision:

- **The religious**–these people, though they may never admit it, attempt to *use God to get what they want.* They have responded to a watered down gospel and simply expect God to be at their beck and call. They regularly attempt to establish themselves as the authority in a church. They improperly attempt to hold someone who has been established as their leader accountable. They are addicted to being 'right', though they are terribly deceived. The religious will be faced with the reality of the cross. They will have to decide to surrender all, give up their dreams and serve their King as he has called them to.

- **The lukewarm**–The Word says this group will be violently resisted by God. Their primary focus is the comfort of their flesh. Anything challenging or costly is avoided for the sake of maintaining the status quo of their daily lives. Any thought of revolution, much less change, in their lives is not at all interesting or important to them. They misunderstand their role in the Kingdom of God, if they have any role at all.
- **The wounded**–This group may feel the force of this end-time establishment of God's government more than most. The very thought of rank and order causes them to flinch and react. They shrink back as they constantly relive the memories of deep hurt by people of authority and influence in their lives. The wounded have never found healing, so their defense is to remove themselves from relationships that may be threatening to them. Unwittingly they have also removed themselves from God's covering for their lives.
- **The controlling**–This group was also most likely wounded in the past. Any number of internal issues can result in one becoming a controller. Insecurity, fear, pride, arrogance and other spiritual chains are excuse enough for someone to actually embrace the same spirit that was possibly used against them–control.
- **The improperly trained**–This group's error was initiated by their spiritual leaders. Pastors will be held accountable for introducing them to a life of independence. Catering to the demands of the masses has resulted in a generation of lawlessness and rebellion. A sloppy gospel and a casual presentation of the plan of salvation have left people without any understanding of God's government, submission, servanthood and issues of authority.

Let me stop for a moment and explain a broader picture and why this book is so important.

God's heart is to introduce people to, or encourage people in a life of hearing God's wild words and to move out in ways that are often contrary to common sense. Human wisdom of old and the established status quo is forsaken in favor of the current Word of the Lord. The prophetic voice of God is echoing through the land. The Bible is becoming more clear to more people every day. We are nearing a great end-time revival! This revival will require precision, quick action and order if it is to be successful.

Those who handle this prophetic movement incorrectly will do much damage. Hearing and obeying God in these end-times is a deeply sensitive issue. Let me say this clearly–while God is about to deliver some bizarre and earth-shaking revelations and commands that will shake normalcy to the core, and while He is going to hold people accountable for their lack of hearing and timely response, *God is not ordaining lawlessness!*

In fact, His government is going to be reintroduced and established at the same time His prophetic voice is resounding in His people. God is planting in people the unction to press ahead, often while our leaders may not be immediately providing opportunity to do so.

God is not ordaining lawlessness!

It can feel like what we have heard from God and what our pastor is allowing are contrary. However, this is so often a part of God's plan. He places desires in our hearts and then gives us an often lengthy humility test by being restricted by our leadership. This is OK. It's part of the plan. How we respond in these times of preparation for advance is critical! Let me say it simply,

Loving submission to authority is non-negotiable and more important now that it has ever been.

That being said, let's launch further into this topic of covens in the Church.

Something strange happened in 1988. The governmental structure of authority in the Body of Christ was violated. Those under authority took it upon themselves to judge their authority. I believe it has resulted in what I call the *exposing movement* that is so prevalent today. People online, on the radio and in print are making a habit of 'touching God's anointed'. They do everything they can to publicly expose their interpretation of false doctrine, sins, errors and weaknesses in God's men and women.

Those under authority have self-appointed themselves as judge. Instead of being accountable to authority, they have removed themselves from accountability.

Wouldn't it be strange to walk into a courtroom and sentence the judge to a week in jail? Has anyone ever pulled a police car over and issued a ticket to the driver? Can an employee fire his boss? Even in a democratic nation we understand the appropriate flow of governmental authority.

What about in a Kingdom? God has established His leaders– and I declare it is time for the leaders to lead with passion, fire and with the love and support of their fellow soldiers in the army of God! The prophetic voice of God must be declared! Many pastors have become salesmen attempting to offer what will attract the biggest crowd and appease the most people. This must stop!

Why has this become such an issue? Ask any pastor, even those who may have a reputation of delivering the more difficult words, if they have shuddered at the thought of declaring certain Biblical truths. All of us, if we are honest, would admit that we have.

Pastors have feared to speak on many Biblical topics like the one we're discussing in this book because of fear of resistance, condemnation and accusation.

Even in a democratic nation we understand the appropriate flow of governmental authority.

People who have embraced an independent spirit often assume a pastor to be controlling himself if he or she is moving contrary to their advice. Pastor's mandate to call people into a position of response is sadly not acceptable to so many. Corporate missions are aborted and compromised due to such a mind-set. Additionally, pastors hesitate to give direction because they fear they will appear to have failed if the people under their leadership don't respond to that direction.

In God's government, there should be NO SUCH FEAR! Quick, loving and eager response by the church should be the norm as leaders operate as their God established authority. *Pastors must resign their position of salesmen and take up the mantle of prophet!*

At this point, it's possible that a myriad of hurts, pains or other issues are rising to the surface. If that is happening to you, take a moment and ask the Holy Spirit to speak deeply to you. Ask Him to remove anything from you that would hinder His voice from reaching the core of your heart. If you have been hurt in the past and have wondered how you can ever serve in a church again, I understand this issue is very difficult for you. At this point, suffice it to say that God deeply and zealously loves you. He knows your pain and has a plan of healing for you. Keep that plan in His hands. Don't take it upon yourself. That simply won't work.

THE 100% CHURCH AND THE CALL TO CORPORATE MISSION ADVANCE

This issue of pastors becoming salesmen has forced the rapid growth of para-church ministries. Leaders of para-church ministries have a greater ability to call those people who have partnered with them on their mission field into a position of readiness and response. The success of the mission is at a lesser risk as all hands are on deck and ready to go. Pastors don't always have it as easy.

For example, a pastor may hear God tell him to gather his flock together and fast from all food for 3 days. In God's government, there would be no resistance, complaining or negativity. 100% of the participants in the church, who had already made up their mind to be unified and ready to press ahead as warriors for God, would immediately embrace this God given mandate. All would fast. If someone had a concern with the directive, that's OK. A good servant won't simply ignore the plan of action, but will rather make the effort to talk to the leader. A good leader will certainly listen to their concerns with compassion.

Much dialogue can occur. However, at the end of the discussion, the two would be 'agreed'–moving in the same direction.

The events of 1988 in Baton Rouge changed that considerably. Now, the process that poor pastor must go through when the need to call the troops to action is enough to cause him to resign!

1. He studies endlessly in the Word so he can 'cover all of his bases'. He is already preparing his heart for resistance–the resistance that was perpetuated back in 1988.
2. Due to this certain impending resistance, he prays long and hard for God to help him cast vision and sell this strategy to the church by giving him 'the words to say'.
3. He shares his impression that God wants this three-day fast with his leadership team, hoping to gain support. He knows he'll need it.
4. He looks at the schedule to make sure he doesn't offend anybody by scheduling the fast during a time when someone else has already planned his or her own event.
5. He prays again asking God for more insight as to the purpose of the fast. He wants to make sure he has enough info so as to effectively sell this idea to the people.
6. He stresses out when God doesn't give further insight.
7. He starts to guess how many will actually respond so he can devise a plan to effectively make sure those who don't respond don't feel alienated. After all, an affirmed and happy family is very important.
8. He then shares how he 'feels led' that God 'would like' the church to fast. Those who also 'feel led' should sign up in the back as they leave.
9. The same five or six people who show up for everything sign up and the rest of the sheet is left blank. It's a monument of a failed mission.
10. The next time God says something, the pastor will be even less zealous in sharing the dream.

Now, the para-church leader, who may have several submitted and committed men and women of God, many who may actually pay tuition to participate in an internship, hears the same voice of God to call a fast. Here is his process:

- Joel 1:14 (NKJV) Consecrate a fast, Call a sacred assembly; Gather the elders And all the inhabitants of the land Into the house of the LORD your God, And cry out to the LORD.

That's it. 100% participation in the work of the Lord. Those under the authority of the para-church leader had no need to pray about the directive. No need to have an opinion on the matter. God's servant has spoken. God's people must respond. Period. No murmuring. No complaining. No second-guessing.

There is a call that I have heard for the *100% Church*. This means *100% attending, 100% serving* and *100% giving*. This call is threatened by the self-governing spirit. I find it nearly impossible to believe that born again, Spirit-filled believers don't tithe. Pastors have soft stepped around teaching this subject to the detriment of Kingdom advance.

A reformation is needed to experience the biblical mandate for a responsive 100% church.

Can you believe only 4% of believers tithe? I read that statistic and about cried and rose up in righteous anger at the same time. This must not be! Extravagant giving is one of the most basic Christian principles, yet 96% have not even graduated to that elementary point in their Christian walk.

A reformation is needed to experience the biblical mandate for a responsive 100% church. A 100% church requires individual believers to live 100% lives and to come into 100% agreement with God's Word and His plan for that particular church or ministry. This is the greatest way to live! Joy abounds, miracles happen, people are strengthened and the love of God burns hot. As we are willing to die to our own opinions and lovingly serve the greater cause, we will watch our inner man come alive.

However, the pastor's authority in leading and teaching such truths has been undermined by a growing number of people who embrace resistance, self-governance and lawlessness. Obedience is a struggle for them. Obedience to a man is even more foreign. The religious, the wounded, the controlling–all those who have embraced the lie of the enemy to live a life independent of authority will find themselves uncovered, alone and left vulnerable by the very spirit they have aligned with.

ALIGNMENT & AGREEMENT

The Lord resounded in my spirit one word, "Recruit!" I heard it over and over again, "Recruit, Recruit!" "Pray for those whom the Holy Spirit is recruiting into a great end time army to war with God in a great end time battle."

I heard the Lord say that he wasn't enforcing a draft. This is a call to a volunteer and responsive people. The willing. Those ready to heed the call of the great Recruiter. Those who respond to this drawing of the Holy Spirit into radical action would partner with God in His mighty end-time activity of advancing His Kingdom on the earth. Those who don't respond, while they may be saved and on their way to Heaven (by the way, we overestimate the importance of the goal of *going to Heaven* and we underestimate the goal of facilitating God's purposes on the Earth), they will not be in partnership with God in the end-time battle, and will actually feel the force of His advance. It's a call to alignment, to government and to being strictly in position, side-by-side with our fellow soldiers.

Joel 2:7-11 They run like mighty men, They climb the wall like men of war; Every one marches in formation, And they do not break ranks. They do not push one another; Every one marches in his own column. Though they lunge between the weapons, They are not cut down. They run to and fro in the city, They run on the wall; They climb into the houses, They enter at the windows like a thief. The earth quakes before them, The heavens tremble; The sun and moon grow dark, And the stars diminish their brightness. The Lord gives voice before His army, For His camp is very great; For strong is the One who executes His word. For the day of the Lord is great and very terrible; Who can endure it?

Every one in formation, in rank, not pushing, in his own column. We must understand rank and order submission, authority & leadership if we are to be effective. Love of God and of each other will ensure we are fighting according to God's strategy.

I recently received a prophetic word for 2006 in my inbox from Dutch Sheets. He stated:

Opposition to the apostolic and prophetic will ... be the greatest this year. He is going to expose wineskins (new or old) and religious spirits, taking off the masks of those who oppose His move. Those who refuse to move in current truth will begin to openly criticize leaders in the Body of Christ that are moving in the flow of the apostolic and the prophetic. Some have been doing so in a very subtle way, but this year, it will become obvious. When they do, God is going to begin to judge them.

He went on to talk about a radical restructuring of the Church as we know it. God is pouring into His leadership new instructions for a new paradigm. The old wineskins won't suffice. People need to be connected and agreed with this new move of God like never before in their lives. I read in another place the other day a prophecy regarding lawlessness coming to this nation. Great disunity in the church will arise due to a spirit of lawlessness. This will lead to widespread betrayal. However, the remaining remnant will be intentionally and passionately unified for a great end-time revival!

Dutch Sheets went on to say:

This is a year that He will no longer allow people to ride the fence. He will draw a line in the sand and make them decide who they are and what they stand for. The political games in the Church will be judged. For those who refuse to flow with current revelation and resist it, you will see them come into disfavor. Some ministries and churches will lose their favor this year. Others will be raised up and given more influence. It is a year of dismantling that which is built that is not bringing Him glory and a year of great building for others.

This is the most important year yet for right alignment. This year, if we are not in proper alignment with leaders, properly connected to those we need to be walking with, and properly covered by those in positions of authority, it will begin to cost us fruitfulness and health, resulting in destruction in other ways, loss of revelation, and destiny. The setbacks will begin for those who are not properly aligned.

Remember the all important Scripture regarding submission to leadership:

Amos 3:3 Can two walk together, unless they are agreed?

The word 'agreed' means several things in the Hebrew text including:

- Fixed upon. Two people are fixed on a goal, on a mission.
- Engaged. Two people are intimately married to one another for the sake of the goal.

The meaning of the word 'agreed' doesn't reflect a consensus, a vote or democracy. Now look a bit further down in the book of Amos it is declared that we must respond to those who are giving direction as they receive it from the Lord:

Amos 3:7 Surely the Lord GOD does nothing, Unless He reveals His secret to His servants the prophets.

God always has and always will give directives through people. That clearly implies that the one receiving direction from God must be confident that there are people under his authority who will carry out the directive with him.

God loves you very much and is capable of protecting you even as He has placed you under the authority of imperfect men and women.

Those under his care must be in a continual state of responsiveness. They must quickly step up. Those called to action will sometimes feel a confirmation in their spirit, *though sometimes they will not.* This issue of confirmation needs to be understood correctly. God would never tell you to independently violate His own established authority. So, while it's comforting to receive inner confirmation, it's not a release from responsibility if we don't feel it. A lack of confirmation is not a license to rebel. God honors his established authority and he calls us to do the same. We could never tell a judge that we didn't have inner confirmation that we had to obey the traffic sign and drive 20 miles per hour in the school zone. We couldn't say that God individually exempted us from that law and allowed us to drive 80 miles per hour.

Again, if you feel yourself struggling here, take another moment and ask the Holy Spirit to speak to you. *God loves you very much and is capable of protecting you even as He has placed you under the authority of imperfect men and women.*

Remember, we are not to be self-governing in an attempt to protect ourselves from flawed leaders. That is the wrong response to the problem. Using a spirit of Control to fight a spirit of Control doesn't work. This is the core idea of the entire book. *As we submit to those whom God placed over us, be they good or evil, God will ensure our protection.* We may have to go through difficult situations that seemingly limit us, put our dreams on hold or even violate our pet ideas and opinions. The situations may last years, but we must submit in love without failure!

God is able to bring us through! Only God can reestablish us under a new authority.

Please understand this point–*leaders certainly should not ever attempt to coerce people to follow their lead.* They should not be heavy handed, cruel or use guilt tactics. It truly is a volunteer army. No draft has been installed. So, this leaves the primary responsibility of response on the shoulders of those under the leader's care. Just as America would collapse if nobody volunteered to serve in the armed forces, the Church is at risk of collapse if we don't forsake all, sign up, show up for duty and serve well. This is the case even though our officers may not be functioning as well as they could. Leaders are held highly accountable for the way they love and lead God's people, and people under their care can certainly count on God following through, in due time, with correction and direction of hurtful leaders.

> *James 3:1 My brethren, let not many of you become teachers, knowing that we shall receive a stricter judgment.*

Simply, people can trust God by responding with trust themselves as they support the mission of the church or ministry. *God will judge improper leaders with precision–so we can be relieved of the duty to judge them ourselves and simply serve.*

> *Romans 13:1-2 Let every soul be subject to the governing authorities. For there is no authority except from God, and the authorities that exist are appointed by God. Therefore whoever resists the authority resists the ordinance of God, and those who resist will bring judgment on themselves.*

The following passage speaks volumes in regard to our response to poor or ungodly leadership:

> *Matthew 23:1-4 Then Jesus spoke to the multitudes and to His disciples, saying: "The scribes and the Pharisees sit in Moses' seat. Therefore whatever they tell you to observe, that observe*

and do, but do not do according to their works; for they say,
and do not do. For they bind heavy burdens, hard to bear, and
lay them on men's shoulders; but they themselves will not move
them with one of their fingers.

This passage acknowledges the dilemma people are in when they are called to honor and submit in the midst of problematic leadership. Simply, unless they are requiring you to disobey a clear truth in the Bible, *do what they call you to do, but do not be like them.* Do not lead others like they lead you.

THE POWER OF AGREEMENT

Let's look at some diagrams that will help bring great clarity to the necessity and power of holy agreement. There is a biblical process that we must embrace in the arena of differing opinions. As humans it is normal to have a variety of different ideas from those we are in relationship with–including leadership.

Just how we handle those differing ideas is the matter at hand. If we are holding strong to our own selfish ambitions (even if those ambitions are good!), and we refuse to place our will on the altar, problems will abound. Churches will split, gossip will flourish and division will actually be entertained as an optional method of resolution.

However, if we embrace integrity, humility, servanthood and the preference of others above ourselves, we'll easily be willing to die to our own opinions for the sake of the body.

When we're agreed, we're strong. In the midst of different ideas, experiences, thoughts, opinions and concerns we simply agree to disagree for the sake of the mission.

Amos 3:3 Can two walk together, unless they are agreed?

Isaiah 52:8 Your watchmen shall lift up their voices, With their voices they shall sing together; For they shall see eye to eye When the Lord brings back Zion.

John 17:20-21 "I do not pray for these alone, but also for those who will believe in Me through their word; that they all may be one, as You, Father, are in Me, and I in You; that they also may be one in Us, that the world may believe that You sent Me.

Agreement must be a mandatory and deliberate position that we all stand strong in, even at the cost of personal comfort and advance.

If God is releasing you from participation, make sure you follow through in the usually lengthy process of transition from this assignment to the next. Don't go if there is hardness, bitterness or unforgiveness in your heart. Go blessed and free and sent by your pastor.

Amos 3:3
Isaiah 52:8
John 17:20-21

·········· AGREEMENT ··········

love

Healthy argument is OK. It's a part of life. We simply have seasons where we disagree, and it's important and appropriate at times to discuss it with the our leaders. Of course, we don't involve anybody other than those directly involved (leaders, pastors, etc.). We don't gossip or allow ourselves to become irritable. We agree to disagree and remain unified.

In Amos we see that God will reveal corporate instructions to some but not all. The rest of us are called to respond to the call of God as given through an imperfect human, and that can be a challenge for the best of us!

But, when we humble ourselves and surrender our right to cause a disturbance we can still move ahead in strength. The corporate mission is not threatened!

Amos 3:6-8 If a trumpet is blown in a city, will not the people be afraid? If there is calamity in a city, will not the Lord have done it? Surely the Lord God does nothing, Unless He reveals His secret to His servants the prophets. A lion has roared! Who will not fear? The Lord God has spoken! Who can but prophesy?

Amos 3:6-8

.... ••- ARGUMENT -•• ....

Here's where the problems begin. We know that Satan is the accuser of the brethren, and he loves it when he finds allies in the fellowship of believers to help him with his schemes of destruction.

At this point, submission has failed. Honoring others hasn't happened. *Personal preference has turned into a personal mission of dominance.*

> *Revelation 12:10 Then I heard a loud voice saying in heaven, "Now salvation, and strength, and the kingdom of our God, and the power of His Christ have come, for the accuser of our brethren, who accused them before our God day and night, has been cast down.*

> *1 Peter 5:8 Be sober, be vigilant; because your adversary the devil walks about like a roaring lion, seeking whom he may devour.*

> *Proverbs 6:16-19 These six things the Lord hates, Yes, seven are an abomination to Him: A proud look, A lying tongue, Hands that shed innocent blood, A heart that devises wicked plans, Feet that are swift in running to evil, A false witness who speaks lies, And one who sows discord among brethren.*

The sowing of discord among brethren is an abomination! Did you feel the weight of that? It's not OK!

After teaching this to a class of interns one of them came to me the next day. He said that ever since he arrived a month ago he has had a heavy heart. He couldn't break through it. After this class God convicted him of embracing a divisive and accusing spirit. He was assisting in his youth group back home, and he wanted to take the youth to a prayer and fasting event, even though he knew his leadership didn't embrace that particular stream within the body. So, he secretly gathered the youth together and took them himself.

Revelation 12:10
1 Peter 5:8
Proverbs 6:16-19

····· ··· ACCUSATION ···· ·· ·· ·

So what happened? You can see it in the diagram on the right. Any idea what word should fill in the blank? Turn the page.

Agreement. *Unholy agreement.* He gathered people to himself, to his vision (a great vision) and away from his leadership. Even though his heart simply wanted God and he felt a prayer and fasting event would be entirely appropriate, his action against his authority was inappropriate. The agreement people had with his vision resulted in disagreement, disunity, with those who were their rightful leaders.

The enemy craves agreement. He knows the power of it. The alliance is so important.

So, this particular individual was in the prayer room here and immediately repented for his rebellion to his authority. He said immediately he was broken and experienced God for the first time in weeks. He cried and cried as the love of the Father rushed in.

He called his leaders in his church back home and repented. They forgave him entirely and thanked him for his heart to make things right.

How amazing is that! No matter how holy you think your purpose is, if you have to violate God's established authority in your life to see it come to pass, you will have to align with the enemy in order to do so!

> *Genesis 11:4-7 And they said, "Come, let us build ourselves a city, and a tower whose top is in the heavens; let us make a name for ourselves, lest we be scattered abroad over the face of the whole earth." But the Lord came down to see the city and the tower which the sons of men had built. And the Lord said, "Indeed the people are one and they all have one language, and this is what they begin to do; now nothing that they propose to do will be withheld from them. Come, let Us go down and there confuse their language, that they may not understand one another's speech."*

Division will lead to unholy agreement. As we allow ourselves to align with others against leaders we are enhancing demonic unity. Unity and agreement is powerful whether it's holy or unholy. Let's endeavor for holy unity even if it's at the cost of our own personal plans and dreams.

(unholy)
AGREEMENT

RESISTANCE TO LEADERSHIP

Keep the previous lesson in mind as we look at an incredibly important passage of Scripture. I've witnessed many people resist authority in their lives, and I've done it myself. The motives can seem pure and we may have the best interest of the body at heart, but it never produces anything good. The story of Absalom should speak clearly to us in regard to this issue.

> *2 Samuel 15:2-6 Now Absalom would rise early and stand beside the way to the gate. So it was, whenever anyone who had a lawsuit came to the king for a decision, that Absalom would call to him and say, "What city are you from?" And he would say, "Your servant is from such and such a tribe of Israel." Then Absalom would say to him, "Look, your case is good and right; but there is no deputy of the king to hear you." Moreover Absalom would say, "Oh, that I were made judge in the land, and everyone who has any suit or cause would come to me; then I would give him justice." And so it was, whenever anyone came near to bow down to him, that he would put out his hand and*

'im and kiss him. In this manner Absalom acted toward
'ael who came to the king for judgment. So Absalom stole
arts of the men of Israel.

Absalom disagreed with his leader, and embraced the others
who shared in his disagreement. We see this occur time and again
within churches. It has a ring of honor to it as people presume to have
the best interest of everybody at heart. However, it's rebellion in its
purest form. The results for those who embrace this spirit are often
devastating.

> *2 Samuel 18:9-12 Then Absalom met the servants of David.*
> *Absalom rode on a mule. The mule went under the thick boughs*
> *of a great terebinth tree, and his head caught in the terebinth;*
> *so he was left hanging between heaven and earth. And the mule*
> *which was under him went on. Now a certain man saw it and*
> *told Joab, and said, "I just saw Absalom hanging in a terebinth*
> *tree!" So Joab said to the man who told him, "You just saw*
> *him! And why did you not strike him there to the ground? I*
> *would have given you ten shekels of silver and a belt." But the*
> *man said to Joab, "Though I were to receive a thousand shekels*
> *of silver in my hand, I would not raise my hand against the*
> *king's son. For in our hearing the king commanded you and*
> *Abishai and Ittai, saying, 'Beware lest anyone touch the young*
> *man Absalom!'*

Just as Absalom was met with judgement, I've witnessed over
and over people enduring long seasons of struggle and frustration after
rising up against God's established authority–even if the authority is
truly in error. It's never acceptable to speak against the President of the
United States, our supervisor at work, a teacher at school, our pastor
or mom and dad. We always pray and support and love with abandon-
ment! A differing opinion should never cause us to remove ourselves
from a place of agreement with these people. We unite with them and
serve as people who honor those God has placed in our lives.

Rebellion against any established human institution is a serious
violation of God's divine authority. We need to know and recognize the
operation of God's authority in all human institutions.

We never speak against or elevate our own opinions above God's established authority. Pastors, prophets, apostles, politicians, policemen, bosses, etc. We humbly support them, unless, and only unless, they were to cause us to violate a CLEAR Scriptural truth. That's it. *If a leader is clearly corrupt and unrepentant then most certainly remove yourself from that person's direct care.*

It's important to understand that to submit to God's appointed leaders in our lives only to the point where we agree with the order is NOT submission at all.

Submit to God and be ready to serve Him through the process of love, prayer and encouragement for that leader. Watch what you say. Speak life always. Do not gossip.

It's important to understand that to submit to God's appointed leaders in our lives only to the point where we agree with the order is NOT submission at all. Submission is actually spotlighted when someone honors his or her authority when the order is contrary to their own opinions, experience or position. We can agree with our authority while not agreeing with the order or instruction or position. It is never appropriate to remove ourselves from a position of submission if the order given is inconvenient, bothersome or irritating.

Since 1988 the church has increasingly put demands on the very ones who they are to be receiving leadership from. This is sin, and it must stop.

The passage in Romans goes on to say this:

> *Romans 13:3 For rulers are not a terror to good works, but to evil. Do you want to be unafraid of the authority? Do what is good, and you will have praise from the same.*

In 1988 the enemy caused millions of believers to be afraid of authority. It's time to renounce the alliance with the spirits of Lawlessness and Self-government and do what is good. Many people who have been hurt by controlling pastors made a foolish decision by *embracing that very same spirit for themselves–the spirit of control.* We absolutely need to sever that alliance. God is our great Protector. Fear of authority will dissipate as the Holy Spirit once again takes up residence in the place where the spirits of Independence and Control once ruled.

Even when the church isn't being run in what you would call an appropriate manner, it's critical to support God's government.

Gary Keiser said,

> " It is better for us to live with a wrong system and uphold God's authority than to destroy a system and thus destroy God's authority in the process. We have to learn to submit to men and not to touch authority in a light way. In all these relationships we have to learn to know authority and practice obedience. We have to know that there are lords and masters in everything; we cannot assume to be the master as soon as we touch something. We have to learn obedience through many situations. One finds authority in the hospital. As soon as he works in a hospital, he has to obey the authority in the hospital. There is even authority in a restaurant. Some serve as managers, and we have to learn to obey them. If we touch authority in a genuine way, we will find authority wherever we go. In obeying the authority of earthly institutions, we are actually obeying God because all authorities are from God. We have to see that every authority is from God. Only a rebellious and proud man is blind to authority; only he will not submit to God's deputy authority.... Titus 3:1 says that we should be "subject to rulers, to authorities, to be obedient, to be ready unto every good work." This is the proper attitude towards human government.... God's authority in the universe is being carried out through human government."

MISSION ACCOMPLISHED?

Many would assume that leaders should make it easy for people to follow. I disagree. To go where God is leading us requires the greatest challenges we will ever see. *It's actually time people make it easy for leaders to lead.* The advance of the Church depends on it! We need to come to terms with the reality that much of what pastors and teachers will present to the Body will cut the flesh. It will require much! Pastors are at risk of experiencing the same fate as Moses. The reason he didn't enter the Promised Land was NOT because of some giants in the land–he missed the promise and was met with the judgment of God because the tables were turned and the *leader became the led.* He was afraid of his people as they manipulated the situation. They ended up causing the death of nearly the entire 'Church' as they died in the wilderness! Moses refused to lead in the face of a democratic vote of those who embraced an independent spirit! This led to his great frustration that disqualified him from the Promise. Yes, leaders succumb to this same inner struggle even today–but it should not be so.

It's actually time people make it easy for leaders to lead.

Moses' prodigy Joshua watched those events unfold, and he learned his lesson well. History would not repeat itself. Take note of the amazing lack of democracy as he gives direct orders to those under his care. Notice how much he looks like the para-church leader discussed above as opposed to the pastor who met wide spread resistance:

> *Joshua 3:2-3 So it was, after three days, that the officers went through the camp; and they commanded the people, saying, "When you see the ark of the covenant of the LORD your God, and the priests, the Levites, bearing it, then you shall set out from your place and go after it.*

He confidently and directly laid out the plan. He didn't sell the idea, attempt to gain support or frame his words carefully. He commanded the people to walk, and they walked without question, murmuring, questioning or the need for understanding. They simply responded.

> *Joshua 3:5 And Joshua said to the people, "Sanctify yourselves, for tomorrow the LORD will do wonders among you."*

He led with precision. He didn't give a suggestion, he spoke with authority and declared what they must do.

> *Joshua 3:5 Then Joshua spoke to the priests, saying, "Take up the ark of the covenant and cross over before the people." So they took up the ark of the covenant and went before the people.*

The priests immediately responded. There was order in the camp.

Joshua 3:9 So Joshua said to the children of Israel, "Come here, and hear the words of the LORD your God."

Come and hear the words of God! God had the direction. The Israelites may have had some good ideas, but only Joshua received the orders. The people were challenged to listen and follow.

Joshua 3:12 "Now therefore, take for yourselves twelve men from the tribes of Israel, one man from every tribe.

Go!

Joshua 3:17 Then the priests who bore the ark of the covenant of the LORD stood firm on dry ground in the midst of the Jordan; and all Israel crossed over on dry ground, until all the people had crossed completely over the Jordan.

The result was a successful mission. God's government, a bold leader and a ready people resulted in a miracle and success. No vote. No murmuring. Precision and bold advance!

THE ABOMINATION OF GOSSIP

I pray you are seeing this issue with more clarity than you have in the past. If you ever feel impressed to go in one direction and your authority has you moving in another, you *don't have to pray about whether you should go with him or not!* We can pray about all of the issues the order brings up, all of the questions we have, but there is no question whether we are to respond or not. God never brings confusion by asking us to violate His established authority. We simply serve with a humble heart. *God will work out the details. The seeming contradiction will resolve.* Of course, as has been stated, dialogue can always take place. Vulnerability and transparency is very important for all parties involved. It's OK to wrestle through the issue, but only with the leader himself (or his authorized liaison). It's never appropriate to bring disagreement or concern to a third party. The moment you do, you open a coven in the church. A place of gossip. It's the enemy's method of issue resolution and it brings division, confusion and an often devastating spirit of Absalom or Jezebel into the camp. It's simply not the

Biblical method of conflict resolution. In fact, while we're far from perfect, my wife and I are extremely careful how we discuss issues even between ourselves. It's not OK to murmur or gossip about others between ourselves simply because we are married. Out of the abundance of the heart the mouth speaks. It's important to have an innocent and clean heart in all discussion with all people.

> *Proverbs 6:16-19 These six things the Lord hates, Yes, seven are an abomination to Him: A proud look, A lying tongue, Hands that shed innocent blood, A heart that devises wicked plans, Feet that are swift in running to evil, A false witness who speaks lies, And one who sows discord among brethren.*

Gossip, which is rebellion, is an abomination to God.

> *Proverbs 11:13 A talebearer reveals secrets, But he who is of a faithful spirit conceals a matter.*

Consider this important lesson regarding how to deal with our leaders who are struggling from the life of Noah:

> *Genesis 9:20-27 And Noah began to be a farmer, and he planted a vineyard. Then he drank of the wine and was drunk, and became uncovered in his tent. And Ham, the father of Canaan, saw the nakedness of his father, and told his two brothers outside. But Shem and Japheth took a garment, laid it on both their shoulders, and went backward and covered the nakedness of their father. Their faces were turned away, and they did not see their father's nakedness. So Noah awoke from his wine, and knew what his younger son had done to him. Then he said: "Cursed be Canaan; A servant of servants He shall be to his brethren." And he said: "Blessed be the Lord, The God of Shem, And may Canaan be his servant. May God enlarge Japheth, And may he dwell in the tents of Shem; And may Canaan be his servant."*

This is one very important story. It's easy to gossip and to talk to others about what we see as improper. We need more Shem's and

Japeth's in the Church! They understood the honor due to Noah and their actions resulted in blessing.

LEAVING A CHURCH

Hebrews 13:17 Obey those who rule over you, and be submissive, for they watch out for your souls, as those who must give account. Let them do so with joy and not with grief, for that would be unprofitable for you.

Yikes! That verse cuts flesh like few others. Let's talk about this, as there is another trend that makes this verse nearly impossible for leaders to obey at times. Leaders are so often pressing ahead in their vision, and the mission requires certain people to be ready to go–and those very people abandon ship. One after another. The harder the mission, the harder it is to keep a crew that's willing to die for the cause! The leaders, so often, are 'forced' into minimizing or glorifying the mission in hopes of keeping people on the ship. They sail into easy seas instead of heading toward their stormy mission field.

Again, God places authority in our lives. *We don't have the option to place ourselves under authority that meets our standards.* We don't self-govern. We submit to God's appointed leaders.

Have you ever left a church? What process did you go through? What did your leaders suggest to you? Let me just say it–*to ever leave a church of your own volition without counsel from those who have been given the mandate to watch out for your souls (pastor, youth pastor, apostle, etc.) is at best detrimental and at worst sinful.*

We don't place ourselves under authority that meets our standards. We don't self-govern. We submit to God's appointed leaders.

There are countless 'aborted assignments' in churches and people's lives. Many people in the pews are actually supposed to still be in their previous church (or the one before that). Their mission and the church's mission, which they played a role in, was aborted. Unfinished. There may have been 10 years remaining on that season of life, yet impatience and frustration and self-preservation won out.

Let me explain. If I worked in a factory, it would never be appropriate to not show up for work in my department and, instead, reassign myself to another department. There must be a process of releasing from my current supervisor and a receiving of my new supervisor. It's up to them, not me, whether I change departments.

The city church has many departments. *It is rarely, if ever, appropriate for anybody to leave a church without being sent out!* There must be a blessing. The pastor's job is to watch out for your soul. He has a great responsibility to ensure you are in the right department.

Here's an interesting question you may have never considered– What if God has given the pastor a specific position for you to fill? As your authority, the pastor may have been directed by God, for reasons unknown to anybody but God Himself, to call you to the food pantry in the church for the next six months. How can he do this if you voluntarily leave his department? That pastor is then unable to respond to God as was originally designed because of an independent and uncooperative spirit. Self-government has kept God's official in your life from being able to assign you, and thus, to make steps toward fulfilling the corporate mission.

I'll say it this way—we do not have an option to leave a church until we go through a significant and usually lengthy process of being sent out by the leaders. There should most usually be an obvious and positive reason for the sending. The new mission should be clear. It should reflect a promotion of God after growing and working through the multitudes of problems and irritants that any church experience will present! An individual never reassigns him or herself to a new church independent of counsel from their pastor—God's established authority must pray and bless and release. Good and loving leaders will take your concerns to heart and encourage you in the proper direction as you both pray and seek the Lord together. It's a wonderfully healthy way to grow from one ministry to another.

Another way to look at this is that we are in covenant with our leaders. This covenant helps ensure that a variety of important things happen in the relationship including blessing, covering, an effective discipleship process, mission advance, etc.

When the call to move to another church is heard, the individual's maturity level is evidenced by the process they initiate. It is important that they work closely with the leadership to ensure the process is smooth, healthy and happening at the right time.

It's the responsibility of all parties involved to look out for the other, to ensure their health and to love them wholeheartedly—even when there are difficult issues at hand.

A Compelling Story

An earlier version of this book was read by a couple who lived in another state. They were feeling strongly that God wanted them to move to Colorado Springs to serve the developing House of Prayer movement. They were extremely excited about the call and while they didn't have all of the answers to their questions (when do any of us have it all figured out?), they we're burning hot with the vision.

So, during this process, they read this book. I met them for the first time as they were visiting Colorado at a conference in Denver. They shared their testimony with me there.

In the midst of their planning and excitement they read *Covens in the Church*. Both of them reported that they felt a great offense crawling up their spine as they turned through the pages. It was hard for them to embrace.

They re-read it and prayed. Through the process they both felt God confirming that what they were reading was what they needed to grasp as they were getting ready to move into another important season of their lives.

What they shared with me next absolutely floored me. They went to their pastor and shared all of their dreams and plans to move away. However, they told him this, "Pastor, we honor you as our God ordained authority–not in title only, but in function. We want you to know that though we feel led that we are to go, if you tell us that you feel it is not the right move, we will honor you and stay. You make the final call."

They saw tears start to roll down the cheeks of their pastor. He looked at them and said, "I've been in pastoral ministry for fifteen years and this is the first time anybody has ever come to me like you just did. You are the first people who have ever asked me to partner with you as you move on. Thank you."

The result? Their church prayed intently for Revolution House of Prayer every week. We prayed for them and were excited about the new relationship that would soon follow. It's the healthiest transfer from one church to another that I've ever experienced. This is the way it is supposed to happen.

An Amazing Update

I am blown away at the lengths God goes to when confirming His prophetic insights. I have been gripped by the content of this book since I first received it several years ago in Kansas City. I, of course, am convinced at the supernaturally driven freedom that comes as we're fully submitted in love to leadership, however one day very recently I was asking God to give me further confirmation.

The very next day was the first day of the new internship that Amy and I are giving leadership to. We met a couple from a house of prayer in the Michigan area and asked them if they knew this particular couple that I shared about above. They said, "Oh yeah! We know them very well!"

We talked a little more and discovered something amazing. God answered my prayer of just a day prior by actually bringing this couple's leaders from the ministry in Michigan to the internship I was directing! They said they have never witnessed anybody leave a church or ministry with such excellence, integrity, humility and honor. They we're astounded at their maturity and decided then and there that they would also model their exit plan when they themselves left. They did so and these leaders also departed in a mature and healthy manner and ended up running the race with me in the internship! They will be teaching one of the tracks each session here—and I wonder if all of this might not have come together as it did if every party involved, me included, would not have been obedient and surrendered to the biblical blueprint for honoring authorities in our lives. I'm still stunned.

CHURCH SHOPPING

To further investigate this issue, allow me to make another critical statement:

It is never appropriate to shop for a church! The American consumer mentality has delivered a devastating blow to the stability and growth of the Church. I've been in ministry for a long time, and I can't count how many times I've heard statements like:

- "We're going to attend 'x' church because it has a great youth ministry."
- "I like the teaching much better at 'y' church."
- "I disagree with the pastor's position, so I'm leaving."
- "I'm not being fed in my church."
- "My current church doesn't meet my needs."

Oooooh! When did we start believing that the church's primary responsibility is to meet our needs? It's when the people embraced control and started making demands on the very church they are supposed to be receiving mission driven directives from!

The church's primary role IS NOT to satisfy us. It's to equip us to do the work of the ministry. Thus, contrarily, *we are called to satisfy the needs of the church* and the corporate mission as the church enables us through challenging teaching and training in a Holy Spirit driven atmosphere. A church is a militaristic and missional organization that has been given an extreme vision by God. Never choose a church based on its programs, its pastor or even its mission. Attend the church that God tells you to attend, and then serve there until you are released and sent by God and the pastor. Connect there for many years! Don't put a time limit on your involvement! Don't assume you are there to change things or teach the pastor all you know. *Let your dreams die and allow the process of humility take root.* God may take five years to bring you to the point where you can be broken enough to serve the pastor of a church of twenty-five effectively—so it can then grow into its destiny! Ask any pastor or ministry leader—*they would take a mildly skilled and gifted person who is long-suffering, enduring and encouraging in the work over someone who is highly gifted with great aspirations.*

I often discuss the principle of the money changers when I teach. The money changer's tables were overturned by Jesus. It was a severe and necessary statement that we need to embrace today—the money changers went into the temple with the *expectation of leaving with more than they entered with.* The purpose of the temple is to bring offerings. To sacrifice. *To expect to leave with less than we entered with.* This is the heart we must see arise again in our churches. We don't look for the church that will give us what we want, but rather we go where we can give. Of course, God being God, we continually grow and receive blessings so we can once again bring something to the altar. We are blessed to be a blessing.

I also challenge people to be full of life, fire, fresh revelation and Holy Spirit birthed knowledge *before* they come to a church service. *Don't come to fill up, but to pour out!* This mind-set requires a great reformation of understanding in regard to the purpose of our churches. We pray, study, fast and grow independently in preparation for the challenge and input we are about to receive on Sunday morning. *Eager response to new opportunities in such an environment results in victory after victory!*

God's leaders have been appointed to accomplish a mission–and God has appointed men and women to serve that leader's mission. Throughout Scripture we see this. Joshua led willing servants. Gideon led. Paul led. It's time the Church divorces the spirits of Control and Witchcraft, dissolves their coven and serves.

What happens when people abort their missions due to dissatisfaction or disagreement? Many these days are arbitrarily divorcing their church families and pastors and starting illegitimate house churches or other ministries. I believe this scenario will exponentially increase in the coming decades. These particular ministries are unauthorized and non-ordained movements of rebellion. They pridefully feel they can do it better than the one they were serving under. They usurp their leader's authority and draw people unto themselves. They are the epitome of a coven meeting. Many house church leaders were once appalled that their pastor wasn't held accountable, yet now as a self-appointed ministry leader, they themselves have nobody leading them. They are self-governing and independent.

Many wonderfully healthy and mission critical house churches do exist–but they understand their role in the city church. They serve and support their appointed leaders–other pastors and apostles in the city church. They are not independent or autonomous or islands to themselves.

> *Ephesians 2:19-20 Now, therefore, you are no longer strangers and foreigners, but fellow citizens with the saints and members of the household of God, having been built on the foundation of the apostles and prophets, Jesus Christ Himself being the chief corner stone...*

CHURCH HOPPING

Closely related to 'church shopping' is 'church hopping'. This issue should be obvious to understand, though so many go from church to church in attempt to *control their own spiritual experience.* They treat God's mission for their lives like a buffet. They take what they want and leave the rest. They assume a position of control as they simply do what they want when they want like a spoiled teenager who hasn't experienced the reality of life in the real world. They are not under authority. They aren't connected. The reality of the 'real Kingdom' must be presented to people in this situation.

Many people today are resisting God's established Church and God's established leaders.

Because of this and all of the issues presented in this book, church leaders have tragically abandoned their vision and are ignoring their mandates from God so as to ensure their church's survival. They have created a very wide door into their churches for the sake of the masses. The masses will be shocked one day when they see just how narrow the door to heaven really is.

This must stop. God's leaders must lead like Joshua and God's people must follow quickly and willingly. God's government is being reestablished, and it's time the Church responds.

As Pastor Steve Gray from World Revival Church in Kansas City said, "You can't get the governor without getting the government. You can't get the King without getting the Kingdom."

ANOTHER OPPORTUNITY TO GROW THROUGH
A TIME OF TESTING

My heart was broken this week when I heard, along with the rest of the world, that Ted Haggard confessed to moral failure.

I found myself experiencing a flash-back of sorts to 1988. As you have read, I was in the middle of the shaking in Baton Rouge that year, and now I once again am at ground zero, this time in Colorado Springs.

I consider Ted Haggard a friend and someone I have looked up to for years. He and I co-led a weekly prayer meeting in Colorado Springs. I was impressed with his humility and eagerness to serve scores of churches in the Pikes Peak region from 10pm until midnight every Friday night. We prayed passionately with anywhere from fifty to one hundred and fifty others for that church's pastor, staff, musicians and members.

Pastor Ted did fail. He admitted this and we are now awaiting the resulting long-term reactions both here in Colorado Springs and in other parts of this nation as well as the nations of the world. I must present this question—will we as the Church respond with love, patience, submission and servanthood? Or, will we once again lose trust and embrace a spirit of Self-government?

If we approach our relationship with our leaders from a position of service, and we don't place inappropriate demands on them, we will find it easy to love and serve regardless of their failures, limitations or our points of disagreement with them.

While severe situation surrounding Ted Haggard's ministry demanded his removal, this in no way means we stop loving him, talking well of him, encouraging him and praying hard for him.

However, if we embrace a spirit of Accusation, that spirit one day will turn on us. If we embrace a spirit of Criticism, that spirit will one day attack us mercilessly.

Church, it's time for us to hit our knees in desperate prayer, repentance and passion. A violent anger at the enemy must erupt out of us. We must ask God for forgiveness if we have failed to pray for our leaders. People have come up to me in brokenness over the last week. They know they didn't pray for Ted Haggard in such a way that would have made it much easier for Ted to resist temptation. They also failed.

...if we embrace a spirit of Accusation, that spirit one day will turn on us. If we embrace a spirit of Criticism, that spirit will one day attack us mercilessly.

Will we respond with exponentially increased intercession for our leaders, or will we once again sit back and wait for the next failure?

If God's government is in place, and every one of us are in position, the enemy's attempts at stopping leaders and the missions God has assigned them to will be cancelled before they begin.

Am I attempting to ignore what Ted Haggard, Jimmy Swaggart, Jim Bakker and other lesser known leaders have done? No. They have done much good, and, yes, they have failed. Holiness and purity must be pursued with greater fervor than ever in the history of the

Church. We must embrace God's loving judgement like never in our lives. And, we must also not go backwards by removing ourselves from a position of accountability and availability to our leaders. There is too much at stake to allow the enemy to win that battle too.

EMBRACING GOD'S JUDGEMENT

I feel impressed to make a point that very few people seem to understand or agree with.

I believe we must pray daily for God's judgement to continually rest on our churches and cities. If we truly understand that God's mercy is wrapped in His judgement, we will not hesitate at crying out for God to judge.

Judgement is simply making wrong things right. At Revolution House of Prayer I pray regularly for God to bring His judgement to this ministry, this city and this region. Simply, I am telling God, "I trust you, I fear you and we all need you to increase your activity here so purity and innocence becomes the standard once again."

I believe every leader must pray this way. If we want God to move in extreme ways, we must allow him to break us and our entire nation. Much is wrong and we can't continue this way.

I know that when I pray for God's judgement, it's going to hit John Burton first. It keeps me honest and vulnerable. I know that

God wants good things to happen to this planet much more than I do, and he will enforce judgement in such a way that causes more and more people to fall in love with Him.

We shouldn't pray for God's judgement lightly. His fear must grip us. As we are on our knees and cry out for God to reveal every weak or dark part of our lives we better be ready for a great quaking! But, in these end times, I believe we must once again understand that God's ideas are better than our ideas. We need him to shake us to our core–so revival can burn us to the core. It's time for all of us to pray continually, crave judgement, love intimately and allow God's refining fire to scorch us.

It's this type of agreement with the Holy Spirit that will ensure missions are accomplished even when it's through imperfect people. We don't have to take control of the situation ourselves. We simply agree with God's established government.

So, let me say this clearly–I love Ted Haggard. I love Jimmy Swaggart. I love and honor God's appointed men and women who, while imperfect, have embraced a severe calling. Humility, holiness and hunger must consume us again. Let's continue submitting to authority in extreme ways. Pray hard for them, serve them, talk well of them and stay in the position God has assigned you to. The coming move of the Holy Spirit will make it all worth it.

CONTACT

John Burton

www.johnburton.net
john@johnburton.net

Made in the USA
Lexington, KY
27 December 2012